Dear Mr. Hunter

Dear Mr. Hunter

The letters of
Vojtěch Preissig to Dard Hunter
1920 -1925

P22 Editions, Buffalo New York 2000

P22
PO Box 770
Buffalo, NY 14213
http://www.p22.com

Editors—Richard Kegler, Timothy Conroy
Design—Richard Kegler, Timothy Conroy
Trade cover design—James Grieshaber

ISBN: 0-9631082-1-2
Library of Congress Card Number: 00-104356

First paperback trade edition limited to 1000 copies.

Printed and bound in the United States of America.

Foreword

I first encountered the work of Vojtěch Preissig, a Czech graphic designer, in 1995 in his book, *Aucassin and Nicolete*, produced in 1931 for The Limited Editions Club. I found the book's design to be remarkable in its complete attention to detail and unusual in its quirky, angular, roman typeface. As a book-binder, I was in awe of how well the book's binding worked with the end-papers and page design. As a type designer, I found the typeface instantly allur-ing but not in a way that would inhibit legibility. As a book artist, I was impressed that all aspects of this production were planned by one man, and with Preissig's clean illustrations boldly presenting a mediæval/renaissance tale with characters garbed in modern (1920s) dress.

On a visit to Prague in 1996, I serendipitously encountered a Czech type specimen book—a gift from my host—that happened to feature a showing of the same face used in *Aucassin*, "Preissig Antikva." As we spoke about Czech type designs, my host showed me the source for his small company's logo: an obscure type design named "Preissig 1914." These two typefaces became the basis for my typefoundry's "P22 Czech Modernist" digital font set.

Over the next few years, I gradually pieced together bits of information about this artist who has for some reason been unheralded in histories of 20th century graphic design. An internet search turned up an unexpected reference to the name Vojtěch Preissig in a very detailed description of one of Dard Hunter's paper-making books. Having worked on a digital version of one of Hunter's alphabet designs and collected his Roycroft book designs, I was struck by the similarity between the two artists and their well-rounded approach to all aspects of craft and design.

For those who are unfamiliar with the name, Dard Hunter was easily the 20th century's foremost expert on traditional, hand papermaking. Among his groundbreaking books on the subject, he is best known for several volumes for which he not only did the research and wrote the text, but also created the design, made the paper (by hand), designed the typeface, cut the type, and printed. His memory, archive and work have been preserved and continued at the Chillicothe, Ohio "Mountain House," by his son, the late Dard, Jr., and now his grandson, Dard III.

On the chance that he might have more details about the association between Preissig and his grandfather, I contacted Dard III. He kindly agreed to search the Mountain House library and turned up a large manila envelope on which was written in Dard Jr.'s hand:

> *Vjt. Preissig Corresp. 7/2/71. A fine artist: we have some of his prints etc. Wanted D. (Dard Sr.) to come to Wentworth Institute in Boston--was later murdered by the Nazis in Czech. during W.W.II--A good friend of D.S. (Dard Sr.)*

The contents of that folder featured many pieces of printed ephemera and the 46 letters contained in this book. The subject of the correspondence was a book project the two were to collaborate on, but which, unfortunately, was never realized. We only have Preissig's letters, but in reading them, we sense his and Dard Hunter's genuine camaraderie and shared excitement in seeking to practice the book arts at the highest level. The concerns expressed by Preissig and inferred from Hunter in planning this production are relevant and inspiring to contemporary bibliophiles and bookmakers alike.

This book is intended as an homage to Preissig's life and work. Special thanks to Carima El-Behairy, Joseph Murray, Dard Hunter III, Tomáš Vlček, Ondřej Šturma, Hal Leader.

—Richard Kegler

Introduction

By the time Czech artist Vojtěch Preissig wrote his first letter to Dard Hunter in January of 1920, he was, by any standard, an accomplished artist/designer of remarkable inspiration and diversity. And his talent and industry were neither regional nor limited in scope to specific media.

Preissig was born in 1873 in Světec, Bohemia. As a student at the Prague Academy of Applied Arts in the early 1890s, he first became significantly involved in the book arts, and more specifically, in the Czech "book beautiful" movement, typified by his illustrations for *Tyrolské elegie* in 1893. In the mid-1890s, he moved to Paris to work with fellow countryman and leading exponent of the Art Nouveau style, Alphonse Mucha. After five years, Preissig returned to Prague where he continued his illustration work and printmaking and was employed in a typefoundry. This experience had an obvious and lasting impression on Preissig's work and accounts for the heightened typographic sensitivity apparent in his typeface designs and his later art and publications aesthetic.

In 1903, *Broučci (Fireflies)* was published. The artist's brilliantly inventive and engaging illustrations make this book even today among the most charming and imaginative of children's books. 1906 saw the publication of the artist's folio *Barevny lept (Color Etchings)*. In 1907, Preissig's prints and etchings were featured in solo exhibitions in Vienna and Prague. In 1909 Preissig wrote, designed, and illustrated

Barevný lept a barevná rytina (Color Etching and Color Illustrations), and created a unique system of graphic symbols for *Slezské písně (Silesian Songs)*, symbols which are used throughout *Dear Mr. Hunter.*

Tomáš Vlček, professor at the State Center for Design in Prague wrote of Vojtěch Preissig, "His free-style artwork in his prints, drawings, and collages shows him to be one of the most inventive and independent artists of the first half of the 20th century."✿ With his reputation as a master printmaker and draftsman of the first quality firmly established, Preissig came to the United States in 1910. After first working in commercial printing houses and then teaching graphic art, color printing, and the book arts at various institutions including the Arts Students' League and Columbia University in New York, Preissig later took charge of the Department of Graphic Arts at Wentworth Institute.

In 1931, Preissig designed and illustrated *Aucassin and Nicolete* for George Macy's Limited Editions Club. It is Preissig's best known work in the English-speaking world, and certainly among knowledgeable and discriminating bibliophiles worldwide. *Aucassin and Nicolete* was one of Macy's favorites, too. About it he wrote: "Whenever one of my friends wonders what there is for the designer of books to do, I show him a copy of this book. Into it, Preissig poured his life's blood. The type is

✿*Fine Print–The Review for the Arts of the Book*, Volume 13, Number 1, January, 1987, p.17.

his, the ornaments are his, every page shows the great effort of his energy and taste to make the type and ornaments look right."

It was from Wentworth Institute that Preissig wrote the first letter to Dard Hunter. The letters, written in English, were penned over a period of five years. So what does this modest collection of letters add to our knowledge, our impressions of the two artists? Sadly, in this book we do not have the complete correspondence, for the whereabouts of Dard Hunter's letters in reply are not known. The relationship of Dard Hunter to Vojtěch Preissig during this time, therefore, remains somewhat of an enigma. But the letters do reveal a great deal about Preissig: we see his personally endearing qualities—great zeal, generosity of spirit, wonderful curiosity, gentleness, courtesy, and a charming persistence.

Preissig returned to Czechoslovakia in 1931, well before his country's eventual absorption into Hitler's empire. Predictably, Vojtěch Preissig was an outspoken member of the resistance, publisher of the anti-Nazi publication, *V boj (Into Action)*, and arch-opponent of the occupation. He was arrested in 1941 and died in Dachau on June 11, 1944.

Vojtěch Preissig's impeccable professional standards as an artist, and, perhaps more poignantly as a teacher, are quite apparent. So too was his unwillingness to compromise for the sake of expediency or convenience. Despite the occasional awkwardness in the language of the letters, the reader will discover that Preissig was an extraordinary man and an extraordinary artist. These letters give us a glimpse into this man's amazing life and art.

—Timothy Conroy

SENTINEL WARNS
NICOLETE TO BE
ON HER GUARD

Illustration from Limited Edition Club's Aucassin and Nicolete, *1931.*

List of Illustrations

Vojtech Preissig ⋅ 258 ⋅ Lamartine Street ⋅ Jamaica Plain ⋅ Mass

Mr. Dard Hunter,
Marlborough on Hudson, N. Y.

Jan. 24. 1920

Dear Sir:

In 1916 you brought out a fine book for the Chicago Society of Etchers, for which a special handmade paper is desired. Would you consider making 750 sheets, about 20 x 28 inch of an unsized paper heavy enough to bear impression on both sides of the sheet, each sheet with our watermark besides your own? If so, where could you deliver these 750 sheets, and what would be the price? I shall be glad to meet any of your requirements for the acceptance of this order. In the imprint of the book full credit would be given to you for the paper. Hoping to receive an early and favorable answer, with perhaps a little sample of the paper, showing approximate weight, quality, tint and finish in which you could undertake to make it, I am

Sincerely yours,

V. Preissig

Dear Sir:

Thanks for your kind letter of Jan. 27. Although it appears that we will have to do without the desired special paper for the present, it is highly encouraging to know that on the next occasion such paper will probably be readily obtainable through your enterprise, and I hope your trip to Europe will ensure the reestablishment of your mill on the larger scale intended.

Under separate cover I sent you some of the smaller prints done here for distribution—I have no copy on handmade paper left of our war calendar, a booklet of 28 pages—we were using Japan paper, most of the time as they were in stock in Boston, on one occasion we used a French paper—the quantities were comparatively small, although we did not use more than about ten reams of different handmade papers a year. If the school orders a special paper for its regular needs of fine printing, it would be larger quantity, to last several years. But papers that you would manufacture for your stock would be in great demand here. We would prefer a good American handmade paper to the imported kinds. The paper I inquired about was for a private edition which I am designing and plan to carry out with the help of the department facilities.

Some years ago I used for similar work specially made papers—I enclose one sample—from the Perrigot-Masure mills at Arches, France (their Paris office was then at 30 Rue Magarine, I think), which, while producing a big line in papers of stock sizes, made a specialty of manufacturing any quantity of paper to order, no matter how small. They had a rule that any reasonable number of sheets made above the ordered number will also be accepted by the customer, at a proportionate price, and delivery was subject to work on orders already received. I remember once I needed 300 sheets of cover paper and they made it. Of course it was not cheap, because of the initial cost of making the watermark. But really the extra cost of fashioning the moulds and watermark is hardly of serious consequence in the making of original editions, and I hope to attempt making some more myself, I wish you could see your way to taking orders for small quantities even. While I know there would be other people who wish to procure special papers for fine prints, there probably would not come too many such orders to interfere with the making of stock sizes and varieties, or with large orders of special papers.

The handmade papers most used by me measures about 18x22, 22x28, 24x34, were in different finishes and tints, but unsized both for book printing and plate printing (etching).

Hoping to hear from you when ready to start operating your new mill, and again wishing you every success, I am
Very truly yours,
Vojtěch Preissig

Feb. 26, 1920

Dear Mr. Hunter,

Thank you for your letter and the encouragement it gives me in the matter of special papers. I am looking forward with the greatest interest to the package of samples you are assembling for me, as I am not sure that I know the grades of paper you have been making. I was not lucky enough to learn in time of the books you made for the Chicago Etchers to secure any copies, and would indeed be deeply obliged to you if you had any extra copies to send me, as you so kindly suggest. I should not fail to reciprocate with copies of the book now in preparation and others planned and anything of my work that might interest you.

I am very glad that you appreciate the little examples of our work here—and enclose two of our posters we brought out recently.

You probably could not yet indicate even approximately when your mill would be running again? I might see whether I can postpone printing the book and await the making of a special paper, which I would infinitely prefer to the best there can be found anywhere in stock.

Sincerely yours,
Vojt. Preissig

Mar. 30. 1920

Dear Mr. Hunter,

I received your package two weeks ago and was delighted with its contents. Somehow happenings here prevented me writing you about it earlier, despite my anxiety to thank you for all those precious samples and especially for the printed sheet and pamphlets dedicated to me.

Your papers are to me the ideal thing, and so far I am able to judge none of those I had made for my editions in France years ago can compare with them. The tints and textures are exquisite and I am sure I do not need anything higher finished in my personal work.

I am not in a hurry with my book, at least seeing your samples I am perfectly willing to wait 10 months for the paper from your mill, and hope when you begin operation you will find it possible to make for me a few hundred sheets more than first requested. Their size would be about 18.5 x 22.5 in., for I had to change the proportions of my page to fit some paper of that size on hand here, when I thought I could not have any specially made. Weight, tint and finish would be like your unsized paper for the Chicago Etchers. I might yet decide for the unfinished texture, which appeals to me greatly. A small number of sheets could perhaps be made light-weight and half-sized for end paper, cover and jacket purposes.

I look forward with anticipated pleasure to making your personal acquaintance on your trip to Boston. It appears you have worked so much more consistently in lines of endeavor similar to mine that I expect to greet in you a "confrere" who can enlighten me on many a subject of interest to me. I have myself been experimenting in type making, though I never completed anything in that line yet, and have on every occasion tried to interest people in the original methods of the related crafts of the graphic arts. At Teachers College in N.Y. they actually took up paper making, even if in that superficial, dilettantish or past-time fashion in which most of such work is or can be practiced at our general educational institutions. I came to Wentworth Institute with hopes of accomplishing in proper surroundings a good deal more than I could previously, but find the authorities, while extremely sympathetic and willing, rather slow moving, and war interference not a sufficient excuse for many delays.

Very sincerely yours,
Vojtěch Preissig

Jun. 11. 1920

Dear Mr. Hunter,

I have some doubt as to whether you are actually back from your trip to England, but hope you are and that it was as successful a trip as you desired. I would very much appreciate an early answer to this letter.

In your kind letter of March 12, to which I replied on March 30, you wrote that it will be at least eight or ten months before you can proceed in a practical way with your new hand paper mill. I then planned my work accordingly, to be ready with my book in the middle of next winter for the printing on the special paper you are willing to make for me.

As I am going abroad for the vacation months, in connection with this edition, and leave early in July, I would be glad to see my order for the paper formally confirmed by you, and the price set, and would pay any deposit on it required. But I am only anxious to insure all possible progress in this direction while I am away pushing another end.

To précis the specifications of my letter of March 30, I will need:

➤1500 of 18.5 x 22.5 sheets (3 reams), quality, weight, tint and finish like the unsized paper you made for the Chicago Etchers.

➤And 500 of the 18.5 x 22.5 sheets (1 ream) of same quality, tint and finish, but sized and only about two-thirds weight of the unsized paper. All sheets watermarked in identical way. Design and position of watermarks is indicated on enclosed tracing. (The angularity of letters is intended to bring the watermarks into harmony with a similar character both in type and decoration of the printed pages.)

Sincerely yours,

Vojt. Preissig

p.s. Also enclosed is our latest poster. –V.P.

WENTWORTH

GRAPHIC ARTS

**EXHIBITION AT
THE INSTITUTE
HUNTINGTON
AVENUE AND
RUGGLES STR·**

Oct. 23. 1920

Dear Mr. Hunter,

Thank you for your kind letter. I hope for the best: that you will receive the necessary appliances soon so as to start your mill running, and resume the making of individually watermarked papers, for which interest is growing and bound to increase the demand.

I am ready to give you six, even eight months longer (until next April or June) for my paper if necessary and to help your undertaking. I am also willing to take over the retree at a reasonable price, besides all surplus sheets manufactured as is quite understood.

Thanking you again for keeping me informed,

Sincerely yours,
Vojt. Preissig

Nov. 11. 1920

Dear Mr. Hunter,

I was much encouraged by your letter of Oct. 27.

In the imprint of the book I intend to make mention of the paper used and would ask whether you would approve of the following wording: "The special paper for this edition was handmade by Dard Hunter at Chillicothe, Ohio." Of the book itself I will remember to have an extra copy sent you when finished.

I am extremely interested in the exhibit you are preparing for the U.S. National Museum, and on my next visit to Washington I shall most certainly be looking for it.

Very sincerely,
Vojt. Preissig

Nov. 25. 1920

Dear Mr. Hunter,

It occurs to me, as the book is not to be printed before next year, that the year in the mark of the paper you are providing should be changed from 1920 to 1921, if the filigram is not already being made. The position of the watermarks on the sheet could then also be changed by bringing them closer to the back fold of the sheet (as roughly indicated on the enclosed little dummy), the names to be only about 2 inches apart, the hall mark about 2.5 in. from the back. This would improve balance in my pages, I find. I will send you an actual size tracing of the watermarks in their new places, should you want it.

Very sincerely,
Vojt. Preissig

Dear Mr. Hunter,

I received your letter of Dec. 27 today and thank you for bringing to my attention the difference in styles of laid paper. I feel the antique laid should be the one used for my paper, as appearing more in harmony with the character of the book than the modern laid.

The drawing for the watermarks which is enclosed needs no explanation, I think. (Size of sheets to be 18.5 x 22.5 inches.)

Regarding the weight of the paper, I have found that I will need my sheets at least as heavy as the enclosed sample, to be able to print the plates, which contain solid black masses and much flat color, on both sides of the sheet without the impressions reciprocally but unpleasantly "shadowing" through on the other side. That is, this sample (yours) shows the degree of opacity of the paper required, and obtained in natural ways, not by mineral admixtures to the pulp as some French mills do. As to finish, I like this "semi-rough" finish, but something slightly finer might be safer, if the finer finish does not reduce the wanted opacity of the paper. So with the tint which I would prefer tending rather to an antique white than India, if that would not reduce the opacity of the paper.

I will need 2000 unsized sheets in the above indicated weight. And 500 of sheets so sized they can be used in binding the book (stand pasting), of same quality, finish, tint, watermark, etc. as unsized paper, but light-weight, not heavier than regular Michelin paper.

But am I helping you in thus loosely describing what I wish the paper for my book to be?

Very truly yours,

Vojt. Preissig

Watermark used in the commissioned edition.

May.9.1921

Dear Mr. Hunter,

I received today your "Watermarking of Hand Made Papers" and "A Bibliography of Marbled Papers," and I wish to thank you warmly for remembering me with these most interesting and instructive articles. I hope you are writing a book on hand-paper making. It will help wonderfully to restore in America this art to the significance it ought to have. I am trying within my short reach to make people appreciate both the artistic and practical advantages of using hand-made papers in fine printing. For some time I have been thinking of asking you whether you could not have rigged up for us a small working model of a mould with cover (deckle), no matter how primitively put together if only it is good to demonstrate with it to our students the making of paper by hand and specially the forming of the watermark in the process. In fact I should like to have two moulds of the same size (about 4 x 5 in. or whatever size would be the simplest for you to get), so that the same deckle could serve, but one mould showing a "laid" and the other a "wove" wire covering. The filigrees could be as per sketch or your own initials or hallmark. Perhaps a pound or two of pulp could be obtained from you occasionally for the lectures. All expenses we would gladly pay, and full credit would be given to you as the pioneer of modern American hand-paper making. May I hear from you soon on this subject? And a word on how my paper is progressing?

Under special cover I am sending you a book in Czech about stained and fancy papers, which probably you would like to include in your bibliography if reprinted in pamphlet form. The title reads in English: *Stained and Fancy Papers: Their Manufacture and Uses*. By Leop. Weizner. With 24 illustrations in the text and 19 plates with 58 samples of papers. Prague, 1909. The word "pestré" might also be translated multicolored, colored, as the German "bruit."

With best regards,
Sincerely,
Vojt. Preissig

Dear Mr. Hunter,

Thank you for your letter of May 11, also for the fine sample sheet with your portrait watermark.

I appreciate the difficulties with which you must be contending in reestablishing your mill on a larger basis, so please do not think I am losing patience waiting for my paper. I feel the book, for which I want it, would be somehow crippled without it. I hope, perhaps by printing something for you, I may reciprocate for the special price you think of making me on that paper.

I am glad to hear that you might settle quite near to Boston, and we certainly wish to avail ourselves of your kind offer to come over for a lecture at our school, while I expect to be able to meet you at your place and see your mill in full run.

About the two small moulds: Please have them made any size you judge best, with the watermarks placed any way. I did not have in mind the regular appliance, if a "homemade" model can be good enough for showing how paper is made by hand. I suggested such small size moulds thinking of the size of the container that could be used for a vat and the smallest quantity of pulp required in it to give a few "sheets" at a demonstration, also the size of blankets for squeezing the water out of the sheets in a letter-copying press lined with zinc. I realize that unless we have a complete professional-like equipment, we cannot aim at producing the perfect thing. I wish we could do it someday, but mean-

14

while it seems to me even this makeshift will be helpful in making the students better understand the fundamentals of the process, especially if a talk on it could be given by you with the demonstration. How soon do you think we could have the moulds?

I am interested to know that you will have a working exhibit at Chicago. I should much like to go and see this well advertised graphic arts show in July. That and the moving picture showing the making of paper by hand is fine propaganda and no doubt will help in securing the success for your undertaking which it deserves.

The book on Color Etching by myself, which you found listed in the catalogue of the St. Bride Foundation in London was published by Hiersemann and is a translation from the Czech original published in Prague in the same year. If you do not have a copy and desire one, I would be glad to get it for you, though both editions are now out of print. I myself have here only a last copy. On the other hand the catalogue of the St. Bride Library would be of great interest to me and I wonder whether I could obtain a copy.

With best regards,

Sincerely yours,
Vojt. Preissig

May. 31. 1921

Dear Mr. Hunter,

I received your letter of May 25, and today came the mould which you so kindly donated for our courses, and for which please receive our warmest thanks, and assurance of our readiness to be in return of help to you whenever the occasion arises.

As you write for demonstrating the making of paper by hand it is not necessary to have both the laid and wove kind of moulds, especially as the pulp needed in each case varies from the other. I hope that by the time our classes meet again, your mill will be in full swing, and then I shall ask you to send up a little pulp to use with this mould, and perhaps you can meanwhile some day tell me the proper size of a pulp container of it, which I might improvise here for a vat as I need something larger than what I had on hand. And so for the blankets, what sort to get. Thanks in advance for such advice!

Later on, when you could attend to it, we still wish to acquire a laid mould which simply by comparison with the other, not by actual use in making sheets, and with a few sheets made by yourself from it and an explanation of the difference in pulp required, would be completing the students' understanding of the fundamental reasons for the varied textures in handmade papers.

I have sent for a copy of my book on Color Etching for you. It is yet a torso as published. I have started several times in the last ten years to finish it, but since the war my

16

work has steadily led in other directions though the German publisher (Hiersemann) is still ready to print the second volume and wrote me about it last year.

I am much obliged to you for trying yourself to get me a copy of the St. Bride Library Catalogue. If you ever wanted certain special literature to be looked up among Czech publications, I would be glad to do it for you.

Thanking you again for the mould and all the help you are extending to us, I am
Sincerely yours,
Vojt. Preissig

XII. TECHNIKA VYKRÝVACÍ

Illustration from Preissig's book on color etching.

Sept.14.1921
Dear Mr. Hunter,

I have your letter of Sept. 9. I will try to get you the desired list of works or articles in Czech on the history of paper and watermarking, and am writing to the Director of the Technological Museum in Prague, whom I know and

17

who himself is interested specially in this subject. It may take some time to have his answer, but I myself am not in a position to compile a list that would be anything like complete, though I am ready to furnish any titles I can find in my library, while I am quite confident the Prague people will be anxious to help in work of this merit.

The news of your setback with your hand-paper mill is exceedingly painful to me. I wish I had the means to push through a fine enterprise as yours. In the first line, of course, I am moved for the sake of my own work as dependent on the realization of your plans, but not less ardently do I wish to see you succeed in the interest of the art in the graphic arts of America to which I myself want to contribute. I wonder if it were not possible to improvise something and start making paper even in some primitive (I do not mean makeshift) fashion buying pulp of the quality as the Strathmore Mills use for their Japan, which I think is not woodpulp. I myself and many artists would use the paper even if imperfect as judged by machine-paper standards, if only the material have some lasting quality.

Meanwhile I would see what chances there would be for establishing the needed equipment for hand paper making in connection with instruction at our Printing School at Wentworth Institute, provided the necessary technical conditions can be had here and you could consider coming to take charge of the work and classes in papermaking, together perhaps with type-making, design, etc. It is less a question of funds available than of whether there would be demand for such instruction in separate courses or whether it would be more desirable as a subject complementing the schedules of studies in the regular printing and graphic arts courses, etc. and it certainly could not be started before another school year if everything favored such a development. I myself would not hesitate. Our school is nothing like the "Wiener Versuchesanstalt" or the Academy of Graphic Arts in Leipzig, and perhaps there can never be anything similar in the U.S. But for the graphic arts as creative art, "Original Kunst" something can be done, if we could introduce all these related branches which by their very nature stimulate the higher conceptions of art endeavors.

Could you give me an estimate of what a papermaking outfit might cost and your opinion of and rather standpoint to such a project as above outlined? Also please tell me whether, when you write "...if I ever get things together so that,..." you really feel that there is no chance for you to begin papermaking at all for a very long time? As for myself I can wait for my paper, in fact I must, because by material and ethical obligations I am bound to finish that book exactly as I promised it would be, and have been basing my work, in many details even, on this paper of special make and size. The question for me only is, can I put things off with any certainty that I will be alive next year, or a second, to complete my work? Unfortunately there are reminders that I am no young fellow anymore. But of course I hope for the best, and so for an encouraging answer from you.

I thank you for getting the St. Bride Catalogue for me, and I will look for the article in the Printing Art to which you are calling my attention.
Sincerely,
Vojt. Preissig

Sep.26.1921
Dear Mr. Hunter,
I thank you for your letter of Sept. 19 and especially appreciate your interest in my idea of starting courses in Paper Making here with you in charge, and your readiness with which you consider and meet such a proposition. I am most anxious to see it realized, as I personally feel it would lead to most enjoyable cooperation with you, and am taking up the matter with the authorities of the Institute. While they are concerned at this time with the routine cares of the opening school year, I have hopes that I have interested them and shall keep you posted on future developments. Of course it seems hardly possible a start could be made right this winter, however much I should wish it.

I thank you also for reassuring me regarding the paper you are to make for me. I myself am sure to like the paper even with some touch of primitiveness to it, it would not at all disagree with the style of the book nor with the technique by which it is produced. With best regards,
Sincerely,
Vojt. Preissig

Oct.8.1921

Dear Mr. Hunter,

Upon receipt of your letter I saw our Principal in regard to my plan of papermaking courses in connection with our Printing School. No decision had yet been made, the meeting of the trustees coming later. Mr. Williston personally is very much in favor, as he is a lover of fine printing and appreciates fine papers. There is only the question of an adequate appropriation to be solved and he will try to get it. He may write you himself, but I am not sure how soon, for there are at this time of the year too many things with the many departments of the Institute left to his mind. But I want to keep after this subject myself, and would ask you to give me the following information for that purpose:

What would be in your judgement the requirements of a shop or classroom for papermaking instruction with around 30 students? What should be the size of the room, the conditions of lighting (studio or basement), gas heat, kind of plumbing for water supply, what covering for floor is preferable, wood, cement or linoleum?

Could you make a plan of a workroom as your equipment would require it—also indicating gas and water outlets, windows, doors, tables or benches or shelves etc.?

Please state how soon after your appointment you could start your work, what salary you would expect (Winter

21

and Spring courses last until March 16), how much time you could give to the classes (I do not think more than two afternoons could be spared for your classes this year from the schedule already applied), how much time to schoolwork in cooperation with the other printing school instructors, or to making small quantities of paper (with student and my help) for the Institute? What personal conditions do you wish to have met? How much about would cost the moving of your equipment to Boston? Would you lend it to the Institute or wish to sell it?

The check you sent with your letter I accept with regrets. I keenly hope we can realize your coming to our School and that I shall have the pleasure of helping you to make here the desired paper.

I feel quite indebted to you for the copy of your book which you sent me, and I am happy to have such a fine example of your book art. Several years ago I was trying to secure a copy of the first book you made for the Chicago Society of Etchers, but did not succeed. I assure you I like the book exceedingly well, also the type. Have you some of the type left at home, which you might bring here for little special personal prints if your class is established? Thank you sincerely for the book and will see how I can requite your attention.

Cordially yours,
V. Preissig

Oct.11.1921

Dear Mr. Hunter,

I had a little talk with our principal again today. Can you give me the additional information, if you do not think my questions indiscreet, about your age and whether you are married? Seems we have started things moving.

I have just seen in the *Inland Printer* your article on Portrait Watermarking. Truly good. The more I learn about the art, the more I want to be doing it.

Sincerely,

V. Preissig

Oct.22.1921

Dear Mr. Hunter,

I had your kind letter of Oct. 14, and as I felt that it was for the best interests of our plans and simplified discussion I took the liberty of showing it (also that clipping) to our principal. I can assure you that he will do his utmost to bring about the desired result. He and myself would indeed be very glad to see you come to Boston from New York provided it means no great inconvenience to you. If you come, please let me know in advance, so that I might arrange for meeting you to talk over with you the question of your salary on which I feel you should absolutely have your mind made up before you talk with Mr. Williston.

I have been extremely rushed at the school this week and you must excuse the tardiness of my answer.

Sincerely,

V. Preissig

OFFICE OF THE PRINCIPAL

Oct.26.1921

Mr. Dard Hunter
Chillicothe, Ohio.

Dear Sir:

Mr. Pressig(sic) has shown me your letter of October 13th, and I am writing to say to you that the idea of our making some kind of arrangements by means of which you give us a portion of your time during winter months along the lines you and Mr. Preissig have in mind interests me exceedingly. I feel perfectly confident that such an arrangement would be a very valuable addition to the work of our school printing, and I judge from what Mr. Preissig tells me that there are many ways in which your ability and experience would be an added source of strength to what we are trying to accomplish, that is, elevating the whole printing and book-making art and profession.

The idea, however, until Mr. Preissig brought it to my attention a short time

24

ago, was new to us, and we had no provision of funds to cover such possibility. As we have no definite plan as to carrying it out, it would be difficult to carry on arrangements by correspondence. If it were possible for you to continue your trip from New York on to Boston in order that we might have an interview, I think it might be extremely helpful. I am writing to express the hope that you might be able to do this.

I also wish to say that we will have a meeting of our Board on November 15th. It would be a very excellent thing if we could arrange our interview before that date.

Immediately upon receipt of this letter, won't you write me again and let me know your plans and what you might be able to arrange.

Sincerely yours,

Principal.

Nov.1.1921

Dear Mr. Hunter,

I received your letter of Oct. 26 and am glad to know that you may be able to come to Boston within the next two weeks, for the season already indicated to you in Mr. Williston's recent letter to you.

Of the salaries here I really wanted to write you before this, but it slipped my mind. They range from about 1500-3500, so far as I know, but it is my conviction that your salary would have to come nearer the top figure.

I have a letter from Prague saying that in a week or so they will be ready to send the list of titles for your bibliography on the history of paper.

Sincerely,

V. Preissig

Nov.2.1921

Dear Mr. Hunter,

I have your letter of Oct. 31. If you arrive here early enough in the morning to have a little rest after your long trip, I would suggest that you come to the Institute at about 10 o'clock so that we may have a little talk before seeing Mr. Williston. He is usually in towards noon.

Wentworth Institute is on Huntington Ave. at Ruggles Street. Any Huntington Ave. car will take you there from Park Street Station.

Best wishes!

Sincerely,

V. Preissig

Nov.11.1921

Dear Mr. Hunter,

I hope you returned home not too much disappointed with the results of your visit to Boston. The shortness of your stay and especially the necessity of your spending most of the time in what probably was rather indifferent conversations I regret sincerely. What the committees and boards will really do for or to our plans remains to be seen.

Herewith I am sending you the English version I made of the list of Czech and Slovak books or articles for your bibliography on the history of paper, as I received it from the Director of the Government Printing Office yesterday. With the help of the editor of "Typographia" he undertook to compile the list, the task having been referred to them by the Technological Museum. Because it does not appear from some of the titles, I am being assured that all the books and articles listed relate to the history of printing.

With best regards,
Sincerely,
Vojt. Preissig

Nov.28.1921

Dear Mr. Hunter,

I have your kind letter of Nov. 18. I am glad you so appreciate that list of books on paper and if I can give any further help in your bibliographical or other work, I shall be pleased to do so.

For nearly two weeks now I am somewhat in-disposed and hardly in touch with the Institute. I am also disturbed in my mind not having heard from Mr. Williston the result of the meeting of the Board of Directors on Nov. 15. Has not Mr. W. written you yet? And I wish to say this confidentially, that I had hopes based on the belief, that Mr. W. can realize a thing at the Institute if he truly wanted it. I was rather disappointed, not to say discouraged and confused, during your visit here, as I saw him proceed in the matter seeking support for the project from specialists who, he must know, are not exactly in accord with his handling of affairs at the Institute. I at least know it, though it is not for me to decide which side is in the right. I also cannot draw any conclusions as to Mr. W.'s sincerity in the particular matter. It is very possible the Directors did not see the worth of making an extra effort as manifestly for the interests of the Institute. But if Mr. W.'s authority and ability involved in the question are seen in this light, a condition is revealed to me that sooner or later will bring about my resignation here, because there is then left nothing that would restrain certain "contributing causes" from forcing the issue. I would not blame the Directors for centering their attention in the financial interests of the Institute, that is an excellent thing to do, provided it is not hampering or checking the man who has the professional qualifications and is expressly assigned to look after the loftier interests, the educational aims of the school which alone justify its existence. But I will see soon whether there is reason for worry.

Thank you for preparing that list of book dealers for me. I wonder whether you would find the time also for a list of books in your library which deal wholly or in part with the technique of engraving (intaglio, not lithographic or surface) and printing of music and banknotes, and whether you would lend me for a short time those of the list which I could not locate in Boston libraries, so that I can make excerpts from the texts as would appear of value. You remember the Czechoslovak State Printing Office has asked me to get for them some literature on these subjects, and most of such books, even if their titles are known, can not readily be found.

Personally, I look for technical information about typemaking and handmade paper—would you include books in your library which pertain to these processes also in the list?

When I received your letter and learned you are going to Chicago (your lecture and demonstration there was no doubt a success), I regretted that I could not write you at once. I thought you would meet at the Society of Etchers. Mr. Lee Sturges (you know I am interested in his fine etching press) and wanted to ask your intervention for his consideration of an order for two such presses. He had written me in October that they "do not care to make up less than six at a time," but I could not get an order for six approved here, at $350.00 each. I asked him whether they could not make an exception for an educational institution, sending a few of our students' plates, without a reply yet. Some day when you write to Mr. Sturges, would you try to persuade him to make the exception for me? I think I could find for him some older handmade papers he may not know.

But I realized I am asking altogether too many things of you. I only hope I can return the kindness and help they would mean to me in some work I might be able to do for you perhaps in connection with your new book?

With cordial regards,
Sincerely,
V. Preissig

Dec.9.1921

Dear Mr. Hunter,

I have your kind letter of Dec. 2 and thank you for the enclosures and all the valuable information you took such pains to gather for me.

I met Mr. Williston the previous Friday, Dec. 2. He had no word to say of you or our plans, seemed extremely concerned with silly routine things and I gave it all up in disgust. Knowing now that he had then your last letter and thus an additional reason to speak up, I feel positively slighted. He is away since Monday, but if he has not written you before he went, I will see to it that you get an answer and your books and prints as soon as he returns. I am writing him so that there be no possibility of evasion or mis-understanding between us—in conversation it is difficult to make him listen long. I am in fact tendering him my resignation. I cannot be head of a department only to be the tool or fool of a principal. It is true this is the first time I have cause for a similar complaint or protest, yet the show of interest as made at your visit here, with this ending, puts me I am afraid in a peculiar light with you, because it was my suggestion which started it all, and it also discloses to me unmistakably conditions, which I had suspected at times but which did not appear to exclude all hope for an understanding that would make real accomplishments at the printing school possible. That my faith in this school should have been shattered just when I believed a positive step forward is to be taken, when I anticipated your coming and the intense pleasure of cooperating with you in great works can only more embitter my feelings of disappointment. So though I dislike, and in view of the state of my health do not deem wise, to undertake the moral and mental and material burdens of a change of positions, I am ready to go with the hope that we may yet meet for a common assignment or enterprise. I have openings enough and time to arrange things, my contract here expires in June next.

I must yet thank you for your readiness to intercede with Mr. Sturges regarding presses. The breakdown of my plans here of course makes the matter less urgent, but I may know soon whether I would not need the Sturges' presses elsewhere.

With kindest regards,
Very sincerely yours,
V. Preissig

Dec.13.1921

Dear Mr. Hunter,

Mr. W. was back to school yesterday and I saw him today. He explained that he is still trying to find support for our paper class idea and secure your appointment at first for the short course planned and then for the regular term. He said he would write you at once and take care of returning your books himself. I can see the matter in only one light and am pained and angry beyond expression in thinking that the best intentions should receive this recognition and have brought only inconvenience and annoyance to you. Of my resignation from Wentworth, Mr. W. thinks it will be time to talk in Spring. Postponing also, but he will have to face the issue.

If you do not get a letter and the books from Mr. W. within a week, will you let me know?

Best regards,
Sincerely yours,
V. Preissig

New year's card 1922.

Mar.6.1922

Dear Mr. Hunter,

Thank you for your kind note of March 2, regarding the paper which you are having made for me. It is most cheerful news. I am hoping it may reach here for the summer when I would be more free to do some consistent printing.

I do not wish to add to your cares by much questioning, but would be interested to learn occasionally whether it was possible for you to arrange for having the additional quantity (2 reams) of my paper made without the "little house" watermark (but with your name and mine), so that I might use it later for some other book or prints, or whether you have ordered only the paper which I need first, with the watermarks in full and as per final layout of Jan.3.1921? Also whether you have any idea as to how much about the paper will cost?

Thank you again for thus taking care of the matter and keeping me informed.

With best regards,

Sincerely,

V. Preissig

Mar.18.1922

Dear Mr. Hunter,

Thank you for your letter of March 11. This was exhibition week at the Institute, which kept me from replying earlier.

I can only repeat that I feel much obliged to you for getting the paper made for me, and I especially appreciate that you intend pricing it at actual cost. Of course I will not divulge the prices you are making to me. I look forward to an opportunity to be of service to you in return for your great kindness in this matter.

I understand now how the taking off of the little house in the watermark would have held up the making of the paper, also why you ordered seven reams. For the book I am preparing I would not need more than 4 reams, as the edition will be small and I already had allowed about 35% for sheets spoiled in printing by hand and there being several colors to be nicely registered. For the surplus I see no use with its particular watermark, but I am glad your name is on the paper as that will make it of more value to you in case you kept the surplus, as you say you can always use it, though I would not wish to force it on you if I can solve the question otherwise and I shall try to. So far as I am concerned I think it right to have your name on the paper because I have mentioned you in the imprint of the book and the block ready, and you certainly have merited what little recognition that means of your goodwill and resourcefulness, without which I could not have had this special paper at all. For its quality I believe the English makers are still much more exacting than the Italian or French would be, having compared certain recent samples, while of course I would have been absolutely reassured in that regard if your plans for a mill had progressed as wished.

34

The moulds could perhaps be left in care of the paper maker, provided later on, in a year or so, he can be expected to be willing, should the need appear to make a few more reams with the watermarks changed. (This change would not require a new wire covering I think if the watermarks were sewed on and not soldered.) Or if meanwhile your mill should be started, the moulds would be brought over. I am "mighty glad" to have a fine pair of moulds and naturally anxious for their safe keeping. But you will know best what to do to that end and to have them ready when wanted.

Do you think the maker will mail some advance sheets as samples of the paper?

With best regards,
Sincerely yours,
V. Preissig

Apr.18.1922

Dear Mr. Hunter,

Your kind letter of April 6 was left unanswered this long only because there is pressing work which keeps me from attending to my correspondence regularly. I hope you can forgive the delay.

I am extremely glad to hear that the paper is now on the way here. Regarding the moulds I think the price is reasonable these times, specially as it is a permanent investment. I agree with you that it is best to leave the moulds at the mill until I know whether I would not need more paper in the near future. There is in prospect a new book, for which I might order another special paper, of course I could not take it up for more definite planning before I finish the one now in hand.

Thank you again for your great help in getting me this paper and for the favorable terms! How do you want me to settle the bill for the moulds? Direct to England or with you? As for the paper, whenever your bill is ready, I shall try to honor in full for the seven reams, though I can see but occasional and subordinate use for almost half that quantity, with its particular watermark. Perhaps I told you that only 150 copies of the book are to be printed by hand, and 7.5 sheets are required for a copy.

Recently I came across a few old bookplates of mine. I enclose them, thinking they may interest you.

With kind regards,
Sincerely,
V. Preissig

Preissig's personal bookplates sent to Hunter.

Apr. 30. 1922

Dear Mr. Hunter,

I received your kind letters of April 21 and 24, and am glad to hear of your progress with your book on papermaking. You know I wish to be a subscriber to two copies of this work, and also of that bibliography for which I sent you some titles if it is to appear separately.

In regard to my paper and the moulds, I expect a payment from the publisher of the book and hope to be able to remit to you the price of the moulds within a short time. I am ready, however, to provide for payment at once should it be of importance to you.

I can see the price of the paper as you figure it is very moderate for a special make, and I again assure you that I appreciate deeply the friendly accommodating way in which you have dealt with this matter and that I remain indebted to you for it.

I will take five reams of the paper (including the one ream of sized and lighter weight sheets—if made), and am awaiting word from my publisher as to the user I suggested of the other two reams, so that I might take them off your hands, if you preferred.

Sincerely,
V. Preissig

May.10.1922

Dear Mr. Hunter,

Enclosed is cheque for $132.40 to pay the bill for my pair of moulds. Will you kindly drop me a few lines on receipt of this note so that I may know that the cheque has come to your hands.

Have you heard further of the paper? I think it should now arrive almost any day. Our vacations here begin in four weeks and I hope to advance the book a little.

I assume you received my letter of April 30.

With kindest regards,

Sincerely,

V. Preissig

May.29.1922

Dear Mr. Hunter,

May I ask whether the paper has reached you and been reshipped to me? I hope there is no misunderstandings about my letter of May 13. I am ready to settle the bill for the five reams at once and, if you decided to send the whole case, will pay for the additional two reams in September.

With kindest regards,

Sincerely yours,

V. Preissig

✿ Preissig's letter of May 13 was not among the materials from the Mountain House.

Jun. 12.1922

Dear Mr. Hunter,

Thank you for your letters of June 1 and 8, the bill and other enclosures. That article in the *Monitor* should mean a bit of satisfaction to you after your experience here with certain people last Fall.

Have you read in the *American Printer* about the advanced courses in fine printing to be started at the Carnegie Institute of Technology? What do you think of them?

There is an element of doubt in my position here because of the work Mr. Williston wants me to do next year, and I do not yet know whether I will print my book at Wentworth or elsewhere. I hope to get the decision this week.

Regarding my paper I am glad to know that it is coming and I gratefully recall your pains in getting it for me. If I had thought of it in time I should have asked you to take out a couple of sheets when opening the case and mail them to me so that I might get an advance "taste" of my paper. I am sure, as you declare it to be excellent paper, that I will like it very much.

I am enclosing a check for $169.—in payment of the 5 reams at $33.07 as agreed—$165.35, plus the freight charges you paid in Chillicothe—$3.63. The balance, per $66.15, for the two additional reams, I will pay as soon as possible. Will you kindly acknowledge receipt of this letter and check? I will let you know when the paper reaches here and hope it will be in the same good condition you found it in.

    With best regards,

Sincerely,

V. Preissig

Dear Mr. Hunter,

      I have had a little vacation and meanwhile the paper came. It certainly is excellent paper. I think it is made of such good materials that even at this good weight it is more translucent for my black type and color forms than I wished. But I can print on one side only of the sheets if necessary. In your judgement, did the makers use any linen in this paper, or other material, besides cotton, and in about what proportion? How long can it probably "live"? Could you recommend a good deep black ink for this paper which would not show through on the reverse nor work through in time as I see in some rather recent books printed on handmade paper. I have a copy of "Fringilla" printed on "Ruindael" paper in 1895 where the heavier blacks not only have produced a strong yellowish stain on the back of the page but also affected the page next to the back and specially the page opposite the impression and even another page farther off. Evidently the varnish of the ink had slowly reacted in a chemical way on the paper in the short or long run. I have some books quite over a hundred years old where the blackest impression has not stained through half as badly on much thinner paper than in "Fringilla." I would be thankful for any hint you could give me as to the best ink to use with my paper. I hope I am not bothering you too much with questions.

With best wishes,
Sincerely,
V. Preissig

Jul. 16. 1922

Dear Mr. Hunter,

Sincere thanks for your kind letter of July 8. I am specially thankful for the information and your opinion regarding my paper, and for your advice and personal efforts to help in solving the ink question by writing yourself to an ink expert. I believe whatever merit there may be in my work when done, much will be due to your friendly assistance. I hope I can in return be of some little help to you in your work.

I have a little experience in the use of damp paper from printing myself my color etchings. In typographic printing, where type was involved, I was unable to get satisfactory results with it, specially in color work, but printing from linoleum, on a proving plate in a hand press, was quite successful with dampened paper, and the present book being linoleum plates I plan to print in this way.

Both in printing blocks and etchings I had trouble with color inks, and could use only a few which would not "run" or stain coming in contact with the wet paper, that is inks in which no aniline dyes were used to produce the pigment, such as the chrome yellows and greens, sienna, umber, the artificial mineral cobalt and vermilion. I do not think duo-tone inks would at all print well on damp paper, though I never tried them.

For my etchings I dampened the required number of sheets about 24 hours in advance of the work. Unsized paper of heavier weight I dipped in water by single sheets, rather pulled it quickly through water in a tray, stacking the sheets up and alternating one wet sheet with a dry one, then pressed the pile—a clean blanket at the bottom and top— between two zinc-lined boards. In warm weather I wrapped a wet cloth around to prevent the edges of the sheets drying up. Under right pressure and with the time allowed the moisture was very evenly distributed through all sheets in the stack. At times, according to thickness of sheets or lessened capacity of a particular paper to absorb water, two sheets would have to be dampened to alternate with one dry one, or another proportion would work best which must be found out for each kind of paper used. Of thin papers, to avoid tearing in the process, a bunch of several sheets properly grasped would be dipped in the water. Sized paper I usually dampened by dipping every sheet individually, very hard paper I left even for a few minutes soaking in warm water before piling the sheets up. Of course I always tried to use pure water. Sometimes I would add a drip of a

% SCHOOL OF PRINTING
AND THE GRAPHIC ARTS
WENTWORTH INSTITUTE
BOSTON, MASSACHUSETTS

disinfectant to the water (about a bucketful) to prevent mildewing. Should the dampened paper have to stay longer in that condition and stacked, later I was rather careful as it seemed to react on the tint of a certain paper, occasionally spotting it. But I noticed if anything has reduced mildewing, the paper also dried up spotted. The best thing to do appears to be to dampen just the needed number of sheets the day before one is ready to print on them to print at any cost all that are prepared, to save sheets from spoiling.

But I wonder whether I am really telling you anything new on the subject.

I am to remain for at least another year at Wentworth. There will be the next season an advanced class in printing, that is the word, but I am in the dark as yet as to the extent in which my suggestions will be actually carried out. I must confess to you that I have been influenced to stay by the certain facilities here for my personal work which may not be provided elsewhere, and I am anxious to have my work on the book now not halted.

In May I ordered one etching press from Mr. Sturges. I wonder whether the R.R. strike will not hold up its delivery.

Hoping your work is progressing steadily, and with best regards.

Cordially yours,
V. Preissig

Jul. 28. 1922

Dear Mr. Hunter,

Thank you for your letter of July 20 with a proof of the ink on my paper. This black appears to be very good, indeed, and I shall see how it prints on damp paper comparing it with the engravers proof black. Yes, I will have to print on a folded sheet (one side of the sheet only), and in this way can use up all of the paper I have, to make the number of copies wanted. Of course I have to rearrange my forms now.

Your method of wetting the paper I want to try. I need prepare only about 50 sheets for a day's work. Though somehow I have a distrust for blotting paper, as it might contain traces of chemicals which bleached the pulp and which mighty affect the stock wetted.

My etching press seems to be held up by the strike as is your paper. We must hope this labor problem will soon be settled definitely.

With kind regards,

Sincerely,
V. Preissig

Feb. 6. 1923

Dear Mr. Hunter,

Enclosed please find check for balance of your bill of June 8. 1922. I hope you can excuse the long delay. There was a series of various setbacks to my plan and only now I am getting again along. Of my new "job" here I intend to write at an early date.

I hope you are well and progressing with your work. Sincerely yours,

V. Preissig

Feb.24.1923

Dear Mr. Hunter,

Thank you for your letter of Feb. 7, the news of your book, and your interest in my doings.

I am glad to know your book has been so well sub-scribed to, and incidentally hope you have me on the list for the two copies I wished to acquire.

I see you did a heroic piece of work since summer and are close to your goal, while I cannot yet tell when I may reach mine, but then, you know, I am able to devote only part of my time to the book. Of course you will get a copy or two when it is finally done, and if you are in Lon-don then perhaps you would introduce it to the bibliophiles there. I hope at least you would find it worth mentioning where fitting. The truth is that I have not started printing the edition yet, as in rearranging my forms for one-side sheets I actually went into revising things, even redesigning many plates meaning recutting. I believe, however, it will be a good book, if new in certain aspects—to the extent as there can be anything new in our line, but I am not sure as to how it will sell.

I wonder whether last time I expressed myself precisely enough regarding my new "position" here. I am still with the Wentworth Institute, but instead of the rather very disappointing and really meaningless block printing and etching classes that accommodated just a bunch of dilettante and fadists, I have now regular courses in typographic design, and though on art matters at variance with the ideas of the U.T.A. campaign of education in printing, hope to get results that will count in professional circles as graphic art. Separately I am sending you a circular, not intended for distribution, simply a bit of school work done by students, comparative beginners, to show you what the courses aim at. The story is Mr. Williston's adaptation of the plan for use in the catalogue, quite stereotypical, and does not exactly indicate my conception and not at all my handling of the problem.

If your intentions to go abroad materialize, I should appreciate to hear from you occasionally and about your work there.

Very sincerely yours,
V. Preissig

Dear Mr. Hunter,

Thank you for the copy of the Smithsonian reprint of your article "Laid and Wove."

I also was much pleased to receive the prospectus announcing that your book will be ready soon. I trust you have me on your list of subscribers with two copies. Could you send me another copy of the prospectus?

The situation at Wentworth has somewhat improved since I wrote you in May. Some of my demands and certain views as to what the School of Printing (now the School of Graphic Arts) should be and do, have been met but the suggestions for a needed reconstruction and adequate manning of the faculty were not thought practicable at this time. However, I have gained the impression that a much fairer and squarer deal may be expected of the Board than Mr. Williston ever made us believe and was himself capable of. So I hope that next year you will hear from the Institute and I should feel truly happy if you were still free and willing then to consider an offer.

I have been in Chicago to look up the Lakeside Press from where I had a tempting proposition. But there would be hardly a chance there for my personal work, and while, in teaching, I can do little during the schoolyear I still have a regular few weeks of absolute vacation in which to push

such long-range work as my book represents. With kind regards,
Sincerely yours,
V. Preissig

Sept. 16. 1923

My Dear Mr. Hunter,

Thank you for your letter of Sept. 10. I am very glad to hear that you have finished your book and (are) reserving a complimentary copy for me. I certainly appreciate deeply the gift, and only wish it would not be much longer now before I can "retaliate." The other copy I had applied for was intended for the Library of the State Printing Office in Prague, Czechoslovakia, and if you could spare one more of the few copies you have left, I am still a buyer.

I hope you can make the trip East next month, and think it would be great to have you settled and working nearby. Of course the change would have to appear of advantage to you first.

Here our school work has started and under the new order of things we hope for more significant accomplishments than were those in the past.

With kind regards,
Very sincerely yours,
V. Preissig

Mar. 23. 1924

Dear Mr. Hunter,

I am sending you, with my compliments, a copy of a Czech text on the making of fine books, written by Mr. Dyrynk, director of the State Printing Office at Prague. It is the second edition of the book which, with the exception of the title page, was designed by me. The book was published in 40 copies by the Society of Printers "Typografia" in Prague. I thought you would be interested in it.

I hope you are well and your work is giving you the fullest measure of satisfaction.

At Wentworth things are upset, a new principal has taken the reins.

Sincerely,

V. Preissig

May. 11. 1924

Dear Mr. Hunter,

I have your kind letter of May 5th. Yes, you did mention the Czech book in a previous letter, in which you also told of your leaving for New York and planning to come to Boston. I have been expecting you ever since, and hope to see you before you start for the Pacific Islands. I will be in Boston until July at least if I am to go away at all, and it is not very likely that it will be Europe to where I go. It may be Chicago, or Denver. You probably have heard in New York that I am quitting Wentworth. The policy of the new principal calls for a low type of instructors.

I am grateful to you for holding a copy of your *Old Papermaking* for me. I have hesitated to remind you that I also was a subscriber to this book, intending to send one copy to Prague. I should like to buy a copy of the bibliography, when it is ready, and think the book on primitive decorative papers especially promising of interest. Regarding my book, at the rate I have been able to proceed during the last two years, it will be at least a couple of years longer before it is done. But one of the first copies finished will go out to you.

It will interest you to know that there is an article on papermaking in the 1924 yearbook of Czechoslovak printers (Ročenka československých knihtiskařů na 1924) published in Prague, on pages 141-150, and an article on the testing of papers, on pages 151-158. I am enclosing samples of a new handmade cover paper, of the F. Eggerth mill, at Prasily, Czechoslovakia.

May I ask you to kindly direct the paper mill in England which has in store my pair of moulds (watermarked with your and my names and stamped WCS &W), to ship them safely packed and insured to the following address:

Mr. Karel Dyrynk
Reditel Statni Tiskarny
Karmelitska 6
Praha III, Czechoslovakia

and to send me a duplicate of their shipping record and the bill of their expenses.

This is the State Printing Office of Czechoslovakia that wants to use the moulds for making a small lot of paper of that size for a special purpose. They think they can change the watermarks in their own mill. Many thanks for your help in this matter.

Very sincerely yours,
V. Preissig

May. 24. 1924

Dear Mr. Hunter,

Thank you for your letter of May 15. I certainly shall let you know if I go anywhere from here (the probability is that I will be free-lancing it for a while), and I would welcome an opportunity to accept your kind invitation and visit you at Chillicothe. I am glad to hear that you will set up your little paper mill again. Many thanks for having written to the mill in England regarding the pair of moulds.

With all good wishes,

Sincerely yours,
V. Preissig

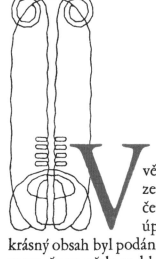

V POSLEDNÍ DOBĚ SE věnuje stále více pozornosti zevnějšku knihy a vyšly již četné české knihy, z jichž úpravy jest zřejma snaha, aby krásný obsah byl podán i v krásném rouše. V této snaze často však se klopýtne o požadavky ryze technické, které mají v knihtisku přece právě tak důležitý význam, jako v kterémkoliv jiném řemesle. Máme tedy již dosti knih umělci krásně i bohatě vypravených, ale většina jich jest v základě chybna; jsou »špatně udělány«, což jest velkou vadou každé práce umělecko-řemeslné. Tato vada vyplývá z celkových poměrů: umělec nezná do podrobností technické požadavky a možnosti knihtisku, a knihtiskař jich často nedbá i když je zná, neboť jimi se jeho práce zdržuje a zdražuje. Třebaže se v tomto ohledu poměry značně zlepšily od prvního vydání této knihy v srpnu r. 1909,

7

Preissig designed page from book by Karel Dyrynk.

Jun. 14. 1924

Dear Mr. Hunter,

I was delighted yesterday to receive the copy of your *Old Papermaking* that you so kindly inscribed for me. It is a beautiful and inspiring book and I am extremely glad to have it. I again thank you most heartily for your kindness and thoughtfulness in reserving for me a copy. I should now get busy with my book.

I am engaged in moving my belongings from Wentworth — there is such an accumulation in eight years — and it will be a few days before I have set up everything in my home. Certain facilities I had at the Institute I will miss, and it may change the course of my activities. But I decided to stay for some time to come in Boston.

With regards, and cordial wishes for full success of your Pacific trip, I am

Sincerely yours,
V. Preissig

Sept. 14. 1924

Dear Mr. Hunter,

I can imagine how busy you must be preparing for your Pacific trip. So, please, do not hesitate to dismiss what I am going to ask you in this letter, if it adds too much to your present cares.

I am suggesting the establishment of an experimental

hand paper mill at the Graphic Arts school in Prague, something like the little plant you have, and like that which I had in mind at Wentworth a few years ago.

Could you then give me a rough plan of the installation (that is a layout of the place), and the addresses of firms (preferably European) from which to buy the special apparatus or machinery (gas heated vat, beater, etc.) that could not well be made or obtained locally?

I have from you the address of the mould makers in England. In this respect, could you tell me exactly what size and grade of wire should be used for the watermark, what wire for the fastening (sewing) of the watermark on to the screen of the mould, and where and under what trade name such wires can best be procured?

This is quite a questionnaire, n'est-ce pas? But your assistance in answering it would be immensely appreciated.

I am still free-lancing it for my subsistence, but may vary the form a bit. I am planning to start a private press and a typographic service with Trenholm. I may meantime go to Prague for a while and help in their organization of the school. There is no Typothetae there to oppose my ideas and ideals. I am working on a set of etchings at present, and will send you proofs when they are ready.

With all good wishes for the success of your trip, Sincerely yours,
V. Preissig

Dear Mr. Hunter,

I appreciate very much your readiness to help in the matter of a handmade paper mill at Prague. I am delighted by your offer to go with me there and help getting the mill started, if we can synchronize our trips. Some time ago, when I was considered for Director of the State School of Graphic Arts at Prague (from a letter received only yesterday it appears that printing circles there are working harder than ever to make the proposition acceptable to me), I had the idea that should it end in my going to Prague and taking charge, I would try and invite you to come and establish a papermaking department. The trouble is, things are moving very slowly there on account of economical conditions which quite aggravate the regular bureaucratic red tape hindrance. I doubt whether an actual start could be made in the few weeks we could spend there. A foundation, some real incentive for action might be provided. I myself could get away only now, before my plans here take definite shape, or then next summer. I have primarily a family reason for thinking of the trip, our children studying in Prague the last three years, but am naturally much interested in the progress of Czech Graphic Arts and would lend a hand in pushing some of their projects, as the professionally concerned want who must be left to influence effectively the government agencies that hold the purse strings. I calculate, if a layout and necessary data are submitted now, and the carrying out involves no very great expenditure and there is no political interference, they will be ready about one year later to open the paper department. Otherwise I am sure that you would like Prague very much, and I would enjoy very much a trip and visit there in your company and hope it can be realized.

Your plan of getting a place in New England where to do books after your return from your travels, suggests to me a possibility of cooperation, though I am not the man with better eyes you would like to find but whom you will easily find in these parts, I believe. I also believe that in Europe, London, Paris, even Prague, you would be able to obtain real, lasting relief for your eye trouble. I intend to seek it there when my chance arrives. In my personal experience, where glasses are needed, they make them exceedingly well in this country but too often fit them badly. Glasses that impose an unnatural strain must sooner or later prove destructive for the nerves, and finally no optical appliance will help. I know that making type is bad use of the eyes, because I have cut a 24 pt. typeface in the last two years (mostly with a knife, in type metal, the State Printing Office in Prague is now casting it from electrotyped matrices), but I do not like to think you have ruined your eyes in your intensive work to an extent that would be hopeless.

I am awaiting with pleasure and thank you warmly for the information and plan of an experimental mill which you are so kindly preparing.

Sincerely yours,

V. Preissig

aáàâäbcčçddd́eéěèêfghiíì
ïîjklmnňoóöòôpqrřsšttt́
uúûùûüvʊwɯxyyýzž12
34567890.·:,;!?"""'-.-—[]
[]{}ɔ×|AÁÂÄBCČÇDĎ
EÉĚÊËFGHIÍÏÎJKLL
MNŇOÓÖÔPQRŘSŠ
TŤUÚÛÜÛVWXYÝ
ZZŽ

Specimen of first casting of Preissig Antkva.

Oct.4.1924

Dear Mr. Hunter,

    I am greatly indebted to you for your long and very helpful letter of Sept.28, plan, blueprints, samples, etc., concerning a school laboratory for papermaking.

    You have gone into the subject so thoroughly, that it seems to me it should be easy for almost anyone with some

58

paper mill experience to start and build up the laboratory. As far as I know, appropriations will be limited, and a beginning will have to be made with only the indispensable equipment. Addresses of German or local firms that make or deal in papermaking machinery and materials can be ascertained in Prague, I believe.

In the folder of the Dilts Machine Works, Fulton, N.Y., which you also sent, I see illustrated two small beaters, of a capacity of about 10 to 15 lbs., that may just fit the circumscribed conditions of the school. I do not know whether these small engines are obtainable in Europe, if not, I would buy one here. Do you think the Dilts Machine Works are still making them?

I shall keep you informed on how this proposition progresses, also how my plans for the future are developing. I have a tempting enough offer from St. Augustine, Florida. It appears a little too far off, however.

With kindest regards,

Sincerely yours,
V. Preissig

Oct. 19. 1924

Dear Mr. Hunter,

Thank you for your kind letter of last week. I am glad to be able to send you the proofs you need for your lectures. I found two sets, one from linoleum blocks, in five colors, the other from zinc plates, in four impressions. The later shows a color process not used commercially in America, since the color separation is not obtained photo-mechanically in it, but calls for real expertness and ingenuity on the part of the worker and means handwork throughout. In France this process is used extensively. The color plates are prepared with an asphaltum powder grain, and the whole scale of gradations is produced by the stop out and etch method. As I am still working on some color etchings, I pulled a set of proofs of one that is printed from two plates. There is not much of a pictorial effect, but the wider range of color combinations and the greater richness of color in an intaglio method, as compared with surface printing, are clearly demonstrated by this aquatint, I think. These proofs I wish you to accept with my compliments. Perhaps you can use them on some future opportunity for a lecture.

When you come to Boston, please drop me a line saying where you lodge. I have no telephone connection at the house. Jamaica Plain is about 20 minutes' ride by street car from Copley Square, but I should equally enjoy meeting you anywhere in town if you could not come out here. As for myself, if there is no decision in the pending questions by the end of this month, I will probably stay in Boston at least until next spring.

Very sincerely yours,
V. Preissig

Dear Mr. Hunter,

Henry Lewis Johnson had me busy last week with his idea of an exhibit of Czechoslovak Printing in the Educational section of the Direct Mail Convention and Exposition at Boston, and thus I was kept from acknowledging earlier your kind letter and thanking you for the copy of your last book which I received in excellent shape and which I shall treasure both as your work and a token of your friendship.

I am glad to hear of your plans for settling in the east within the next year, and should like to think that it might then be possible for us to cooperate on some books or otherwise.

At the Convention I met Goudy and Gress, and they told me that you are soon to leave on your intended South Sea trip. I hope you will enjoy it, and find enough of the material you want to collect.

Last Christmas when Mrs. Hunter informed me of your eye trouble and I wrote you to Columbus, I did not realize it was so serious. And when later on I learned that you are going to England I felt sure you had completely recovered. So I was painfully surprised by your postscript that there is a grave consequence to the accident, but am reassured by the philosophic way in which you are meeting the situation.

With all good wishes,

Sincerely yours,
V. Preissig

Please note the change of address
after August 12, 1931, of Vojtech Preissig
to
PRAHA-SPORILOV 62-8
Czechoslovakia
Europe

Regards and all
good wishes!

Vojt Preissig

Colophon

This book was printed offset on CLASSIC® laid paper from Neenah Paper by Petit Printing and set in 12 point Preissig Roman with Preissig Ornaments from P22 type foundry and *Růžina Italic* from Psy/Ops type foundry. The ornaments used at the end of each letter originally appeared in the book *Slezské písné* by Petr Bezruč, 1909. This book was produced in its entirety in Buffalo, New York. An edition of 1000 copies is perfect bound. A special edition numbered 1-50 is hand sewn and quarter bound in leather with decorative screen printed papers by Abaca Press and additional letterpressed sheets hand printed at Paradise Press. The watermarked handmade paper was produced at the Moutain House Paper Mill by Dard Hunter III Chillicothe Ohio

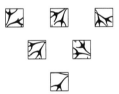